ELLEN DEGENERES:

FROM COMEDY CLUB TO TALK SHOW

EXTRAORDINARY SUCCESS WITH A HIGH SCHOOL DIPLOMA OR LESS

JENNIFER ANISTON: FROM FRIENDS TO FILMS

TYRA BANKS: FROM THE RUNWAY TO THE TELEVISION SCREEN

HALLE BERRY: FROM BEAUTY QUEEN TO OSCAR WINNER

JAMES CAMERON: FROM TRUCK DRIVER TO DIRECTOR

SIMON COWELL: FROM THE MAILROOM TO IDOL FAME

ELLEN DEGENERES: FROM COMEDY CLUB TO TALK SHOW

MICHAEL DELL: FROM CHILD ENTREPRENEUR TO COMPUTER MAGNATE

STEVE JOBS: FROM APPLES TO APPS

RACHAEL RAY: FROM CANDY COUNTER TO COOKING SHOW

RUSSELL SIMMONS: FROM THE STREETS TO THE MUSIC BUSINESS

JIM SKINNER: FROM BURGERS TO THE BOARDROOM

HARRY TRUMAN: FROM FARMER TO PRESIDENT

MARK ZUCKERBERG: FROM FACEBOOK TO FAMOUS

ELLEN DEGENERES:

FROM COMEDY CLUB TO TALK SHOW

by Jaime Seba

Mason Crest

ELLEN DEGENERES: *FROM COMEDY CLUB TO TALK SHOW*

Mason Crest
370 Reed Road
Broomall, Pennsylvania 19008
www.masoncrest.com

Printed and bound in the United States of America.

First printing
9 8 7 6 5 4 3 2 1

Library of Congress Cataloging-in-Publication Data

Seba, Jaime.
    Ellen DeGeneres : from comedy club to talk show / by Jaime Seba.
        p. cm. — (Extraordinary success with a high school diploma or less)
    Includes index.
    ISBN 978-1-4222-2297-3 (hardcover) — ISBN 978-1-4222-2293-5 (series hardcover)— ISBN 978-1-4222-9358-4 (ebook)
1. DeGeneres, Ellen—Juvenile literature. 2. Comedians—United States—Biography—Juvenile literature. 3. Television personalities—United States—Biography—Juvenile literature. I. Title.
    PN2287.D358S43 2012
    792.702'8092—dc22
    [B]
                                                2011001862

Produced by Harding House Publishing Services, Inc.
www.hardinghousepages.com
Interior design by Camden Flath
Cover design by Torque Advertising + Design.

CONTENTS

INTRODUCTION

Finding a great job without a college degree is hard to do—but it's possible. In fact, more and more, going to college doesn't necessarily guarantee you a job. In the past few years, only one in four college graduates find jobs in their field. And, according to the U.S. Bureau of Labor Statistics, eight out of the ten fastest-growing jobs don't require college degrees.

But that doesn't mean these jobs are easy to get. You'll need to be willing to work hard. And you'll also need something else. The people who build a successful career without college are all passionate about their work. They're excited about it. They're committed to getting better and better at what they do. They don't just want to make money. They want to make money doing something they truly love.

So a good place for you to start is to make a list of the things you find really interesting. What excites you? What do you love doing? Is there any way you could turn that into a job?

Now talk to people who already have jobs in that field. How did they get where they are today? Did they go to college—or did they find success through some other route? Do they know anyone else you can talk to? Talk to as many people as you can to get as many perspectives as possible.

According to the U.S. Department of Labor, two out of every three jobs require on-the-job training rather than a college degree. So your next step might be to find an entry-level position in the field that interests you. Don't expect to start at the top. Be willing to learn while you work your way up from the bottom.

That's what almost all the individuals in this series of books did: they started out somewhere that probably seemed pretty distant from their end goal—but it was actually the first step in their journey. Celebrity Simon Cowell began his career working in a mailroom. Jim Skinner, who ended up running McDonald's Corporation, started out flipping burgers. World-famous cook Rachael Ray worked at a candy counter. All these people found incredible success without a college degree—but they all had a dream of where they wanted to go in life . . . and they were willing to work hard to make their dream real.

Ask yourself: Do I have a dream? Am I willing to work hard to make it come true? The answers to those questions are important!

CHAPTER 1
A DIFFERENT
KIND OF SUCCESS

Words to Know

embodies: Embodies means that something is represented in a visible form.

humanitarian: Humanitarian has to do with working to help other people have better lives.

icon: An icon is a symbol or emblem.

perserverance: Perseverance is the ability to stick with something and not give up.

advocate: An advocate is someone who speaks out on behalf of a cause, another person, or a group of people.

In 2009, a crowd of eager graduating college students at Tulane University in New Orleans, Louisiana, hushed as they awaited the arrival of their famous commencement speaker.

"How does one introduce a woman who is on a first-name basis with the world?" said Tulane President Scott Cowen. He went on to say:

Mention that Ellen is speaking at your ceremony, and everyone instantly knows to whom you are referring. Yet one feels compelled to mention her twelve Emmys, her hosting of the Academy Awards, her career as a standup comedian, and her daily hosting of an award-wining TV series, *The Ellen DeGeneres Show.* And, of course, her dancing.

Moments later, Ellen DeGeneres stepped to the podium as the audience cheered wildly. The then-51-year-old comedian and television star found herself in a place she never expected to be. And of course, she made a joke out of it.

"I didn't go to college here," Ellen told the crowd. "And I didn't go to college at all, any college. And I'm not saying you wasted your time or money, but look at me—I'm a huge celebrity."

But in spite of her lack of education, her presence at the university that day made perfect sense. The graduates were from the so-called Katrina Class. As first-year students, they were on campus just hours before being forced to evacuate when Hurricane Katrina threatened the historic city in 2005. The crippling storm flooded 70 percent of the Tulane University campus, caused more than $650 million in damages, and shut down the university for the entire semester.

Ellen had also appeared at the college's commencement ceremony in 2006, when former Presidents George H.W. Bush and Bill Clinton spoke to the graduates whose final semester had seen them scattered to neighboring universities in the wake of the natural disaster. Ellen, who was born in New Orleans, had come to the aid of the distraught city. In recognition of her

Hurricane Katrina was devastating for the city of New Orleans and people throughout the Gulf Coast.

Many people lost everything in Hurricane Katrina. Ellen's worked hard to use her success to help people who were hurt by the hurricane.

efforts, Tulane University bestowed upon her the prestigious Presidential Medal."

"After Katrina, New Orleaneans needed help, and Ellen DeGeneres was quick to use her fame to remind the world that New Orleans was her city, too," Tulane President Cowen said.

> Through her, America saw the tragedy more personally. Ellen raised millions of dollars for the city and its citizens. She raised the consciousness of an entire country, and she has continued to use her bully pulpit to put a human face on the suffering and devastation that occurred here. . . . Ellen *embodies* the culture, the heritage, and the spirit of this magnificent city, and I am pleased to present Ellen DeGeneres with Tulane's Presidential Medal.

The resurgence of New Orleans following the catastrophic 2005 storm shared many similarities with Ellen's life. After a series of challenging pitfalls in her early years, Ellen recovered from a horrible personal tragedy that became a springboard to a career that allows her to use her opinions, passions, and razor-sharp wit to call attention to some of the most important cultural and *humanitarian* issues of her time.

Speaking to the students at Tulane University, Ellen acknowledged that while she didn't have a formal college education, she had learned from the School of Hard Knocks—the lessons learned from years of experiencing many professional and personal highs and lows. But, she repeatedly told them, she learned from her experiences.

Some of the lessons of her life came from her parents' divorce, her mother's cancer diagnosis, a grueling battle with abuse, a tragic death, and then coming out as gay on the national landscape, which threatened to destroy the career she had fought so hard to build.

Despite all of those trials, Ellen worked to develop herself into a cultural *icon* and role model. Today, she is a sparkling example of success through *perseverance* in American culture. She has graced the covers of numerous national magazines, appeared in national commercials, won hearts with two television sitcoms, and lent her voice to the beloved Dory in Disney/Pixar's smash hit *Finding Nemo*. She was even featured in a ride at Walt Disney World's EPCOT Park, Ellen's Energy World.

After achieving her celebrity status, Ellen could have just enjoyed her personal success, the way so many other famous people in popular culture do. Instead, she's used her incredible influence to give back to her many communities. As a Louisiana native, she was an outspoken *advocate* for the rebuilding of New Orleans. In her role as a leader to the gay community, she gave several emotional pleas on her show to put a stop to anti-gay violence and a wave of suicides among gay young people in 2010. An animal-lover since childhood, she raised money and awareness to stop animal cruelty. In a sign of devotion to her beloved mother, Betty, she dedicated a month of her shows to raising money for breast cancer research, dowsing a parade of celebrities in a dunk

Ellen's worked to support breast cancer awareness and raise money to find a cure.

tank. Actress Minnie Driver, NBA star Tony Parker, singer Sheryl Crow, and actress Julia Louis Dreyfus were among the many stars who took the plunge, earning $10,000 each for the Susan G. Komen for the Cure breast cancer organization. Ellen also featured breast cancer survivors on her website, sharing personal stories and recognizing ordinary citizens who had made efforts to raise money and awareness for the disease.

And Ellen clearly values the importance of a college education. She's arranged for thousands of dollars in scholarship money for young people across the country. In May 2009, she selected audience member Karen Johnson as the recipient of a daily $1,000 prize. Johnson, who Ellen told the audience was

Ellen's mother raised a family and survived breast cancer. Her spirit drives Ellen to succeed and help others.

working three jobs to pay off students loans and had to decline her acceptance to Johns Hopkins University for graduate school because she couldn't afford it, was overwhelmed and sobbing at the unexpected surprise. But that was nothing compared to Ellen's next announcement.

"There's a lot of people out there that are struggling, and for you to be working three jobs, and to try to keep going like this, that's got to be really frustrating," Ellen told Johnson. "We want to make sure you go, so . . . we're going to give you this $15,000 scholarship. You're going to school!"

CHAPTER 2
SCHOOL YEARS

Words to Know

propensity: A propensity is a natural inclination or preference for something.

mastectomy: A mastectomy is the surgical removal of a breast.

Born in New Orleans, Louisiana, in 1958, Ellen DeGeneres lived with her parents and older brother, Vance. Her parents, Betty and Elliott, were devout Christian Scientists, and they gave their children a supportive upbringing.

She loved the city and spent her childhood exploring the exciting area. And she truly appreciated life in the "The Big Easy."

"I rode my bike everywhere, all over the campus (of Newcomb College, part of Tulane University), all over uptown," Ellen said. "You know, people can grow up in New Orleans without realizing how unique a city it is. I remember thinking that it was a really neat place."

As a student at La Salle Elementary School, her personality didn't yet reflect the dynamic and exciting performer she would one day be.

"She wasn't a show-off or a class clown or even all that funny—really sort of average," said a former classmate. "La Salle was a small neighborhood school, the kind of place where everybody knew everybody. We'd go over to each other's house for birthday parties or to play, and Ellen's family was no different from the rest. There was nothing that made them stand out in your memory."

Ellen also loved animals and idolized famed zoologist Dian Fossey, who had spent years studying gorillas in the mountain forests of Rwanda. She dreamed of becoming a naturalist, an expert in natural history, or joining the Peace Corps, a group of volunteers who travel overseas to help improve and enhance the lives of people in need.

Like many others of her generation, Ellen also drew inspiration from the television shows of the 1960s, like *The Ed Sullivan Show*, *The Dick Van Dyke Show*, and *I Love Lucy*. Though she didn't understand it at the time, she started to recognize some similarities between herself and the people she watched on television.

"When I was a kid, I would always watch stand-up comics really closely, like on *The Ed Sullivan Show*, no matter who they were," she said. "It must have been a subconscious thing because at the time I had no idea that I wanted to be a comic."

Although her family was loving and people in the community regarded them fondly, inside the home, all was not well. The family struggled to communicate, even about positive things. And there was no discussion about anything negative or challenging.

Ed Sullivan's television show inspired Ellen when she was young.

"The DeGenereses just were not big talkers in the house," older brother Vance said. "You didn't talk about things."

Both children were very aware of the unhappiness in their home. It created in them the desire to have a very different life. "[I was] afraid of anything; my experience was denial about real feelings, denial about pure joy and crazy, screaming happiness," Ellen said.

> There was no anger and screaming lows. But I'm really grateful for everything that I went through because [I decided] this is what I had to overcome. I was going to take chances. I was going to be different. I was going to be successful. I was going to have money.

As a result of the strains in the home, Betty and Elliott decided to end their marriage when Betty chose to relocate to Metairie, Louisiana. After her parents' divorce in 1970, Ellen, then thirteen, began to use her funny personality to help someone else—her mother, who was struggling to cope with the drastic life change.

"My mother was going through some really hard times, and I could see when she was really getting down, and I would start to make fun of her dancing," Ellen said.

> Then she'd start to laugh and I'd make fun of her laughing. And she'd laugh so hard she'd start to cry, and then I'd make fun of that. So I would totally bring her from

where I'd seen her start going into depression to all the way out of it.

She began to see the magic of her talent for comedy. She started to see what it could bring to other people.

"I was helping [my mother] cope with a broken heart," Ellen told *Teen People* in 2006. "It brought us closer together and made me realize the power of humor."

But Ellen also struggled with the difficulties of the situation in her own way. Though she had always been a well-behaved child, by age sixteen she gave in to peer pressure from her friends at Grace King High School in Metairie. She stayed out late, drank beer, and got into trouble. Her mother was worried.

Within a few years, Betty remarried. Ellen moved with her mother and stepfather to Atlanta, Texas, where they sought to make a fresh start. Though Ellen stopped her bad behavior, she wasn't comfortable or satisfied in Atlanta. She called it a "confining atmosphere" and struggled to find her place.

"She was really rather quiet in class, but she had a shy, sly grin," said her English teacher, Ruth Trumble. "Even though Ellen didn't say much, I could tell her mind was always working."

Throughout her life, Ellen had admired and adored her older brother, Vance. In 1977, he began to attract attention with his band Dark Ages, which performed in New Orleans. Ellen saw the attention and popularity that came with being well known, and she wanted to experience that excitement too.

"Everybody knew who he was," Ellen said. "That's what motivated me to do something, because I watched him get all this attention and glory."

At Atlanta High School, she played on the tennis team and became popular among her classmates. And she began to share her personality with the people around her.

"Ellen was impulsive in a very warm and charming way," said her former teacher Sidney Harris. "She had no trouble making friends quickly, and she had no trouble keeping them. Nor can I recall her ever saying a cross word about anyone. . . . She had a **propensity** for finding the comical in everything."

But things in her personal life were far from comical. When she was sixteen, her mother was diagnosed with breast cancer.

"Everything was a dirty little secret back then," Ellen said about that time. "The fact that she had a **mastectomy** was not spoken of. She tried to shield me from it a little bit, but she needed my help with recovery and physical rehabilitation. It bonded us even more."

Ellen devoted her time and energy to caring for her mother and helping her return to health. And while that strengthened the relationship between mother and daughter, another dark cloud entered her life. While her mother recovered from her life-threatening illness, Ellen's stepfather began to sexually abuse her.

Not wanting to burden her mother with additional problems while she recovered from cancer, Ellen suffered in silence before

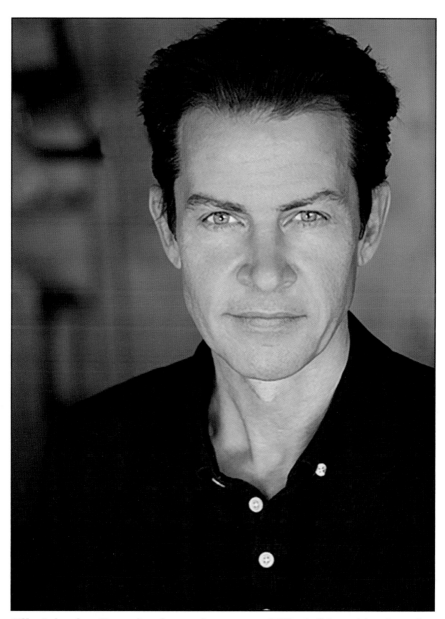

Ellen's brother Vance has been a huge part of Ellen's life and her incredible success.

finding a way to leave the damaging situation. After graduating from Atlanta High School in 1976, she returned to New Orleans, which she always felt was her home. She attended the University of New Orleans as a communications major, but dropped out after one semester.

> I hate school, but I started college because everyone else was going. . . . I just remember sitting in there and they were talking about the history of the Greek theatre or something and thinking, "This is not what I want to know."

Years later, in 2009, Ellen spoke about this challenging decision in her commencement address at Tulane University. "When I finished school, I was completely lost," Ellen told the group.

> And by "school" I mean middle school. But I went ahead and finished high school, anyway. And I really had no ambition. I didn't know what I wanted to do. I did everything. . . . I shucked oysters. I was a hostess. I was a bartender. I was a waitress. I painted houses. I sold vacuum cleaners. I had no idea, and I thought I'd just finally settle on some job, and I would make enough money to pay my rent, maybe have basic cable, maybe not. I didn't really have a plan. My point is that by the time I was your age, I really thought I knew who I was. But I had no idea. . . . I had no idea what I wanted to do with my life.

She also worked at a law firm, but left when she couldn't tolerate the dress code. After numerous other jobs, including a retail clothing store, she yearned for independence and the ability to express herself.

"I actually liked my first job," Ellen said.

I was driving cars out of a car wash, you know, once the car comes out, you get in and you wipe it. That was exciting to me to drive the nice cars. . . . The worst job I ever had—and it lasted a half a day—was I worked in a glove

Ellen enrolled at the University of New Orleans, but she didn't stay at college long.

One of Ellen's first jobs was working at a car wash. She might not have known it then, but she was on a path to bigger things!

factory in Atlanta, Texas. It was horrible. I was checking for too many fingers or a hole or something, and gloves would just go by. . . . Everything I did was a nine-to-five job I hated. . . . I worked in a law firm. I was a court runner. I just hated being in an office.

When she was twenty-one, Ellen began a relationship with poet Kathy Perkoff. After years of struggling with her sexuality, she had finally accepted herself as a lesbian. Her relationship with Kathy was healthy and happy. "They were two very creative people, crazy and young and very much in love," said Perkoff's sister, Rachel.

But once again, a tragic and life-shattering incident would change the course of Ellen's life.

O

THE
MAG

LIVE YOUR BE LI

Ooprah!

**YOU'VE GOT
THE POWER!**
Master the art
of being lucky

What Ellen DeGeneres
Knows for Sure (She *Thinks*),
Page 225

"THE SECRET TO REAL
HAPPINESS IS SHARING IT."
—OPRAH

**80 Inspiring Ways to
Get Your Glow On**
Our Gifts to You: Perfect Party Dresses (for $40!),
Can't-Put-Down Books, Decadent Recipes, Soulful Journeys...

(Wait, that's not all)

CHAPTER 3
RISE TO SUCCESS

"The way I ended up on this path was from a very tragic event," Ellen DeGeneres told the audience at the 2009 Tulane University commencement. "My girlfriend at the time was killed in a car accident. And I passed the accident, and I didn't know it was her, and I kept going. And I found out shortly after that it was her."

The car accident victim was Kathy Perkoff. Her death sent Ellen into a tailspin and led her to thoroughly analyze her life and the direction she was going.

"I was living in a basement apartment," Ellen said.

> I had no money. I had no heat, no air. I had a mattress on
> the floor, and the apartment was infested with fleas. And
> I was soul-searching. I was like, "Why is she suddenly
> gone, and there are fleas here? I don't understand. There
> must be a purpose."

She began to contemplate the world around her. She thought
about what she wanted to take from it and bring to it. She was
searching for answers, but she couldn't find any.

"Wouldn't it be so convenient if we could just pick up the
phone and call God and ask these questions?" Ellen said.

> And I started writing. And what poured out of me was an
> imaginary conversation with God, which was one-sided.
> And I finished writing it, and I looked at it, and I said
> to myself—and I hadn't even been doing standup, ever,
> there was no club in town—I said, "I'm going to do this
> on *The Tonight Show* with Johnny Carson." At the time
> he was the king. "And I'm going to be the first woman
> in the history of the show to be called over to sit down."
> And several years later, I was the first woman in the
> history of the show, and only woman in the history of
> the show, to sit down because of that phone conversation
> with God that I wrote.

She wrote the piece, called "A Phone Call to God," about her
struggle to understand mortality. Afterward, Ellen, then twenty-

Ellen dreamed of performing on Johnny Carson's show.

three, started writing comedy material. She began performing for friends, and then expanded to local coffeehouses and comedy clubs. Eventually, she earned the role of master of ceremonies at Clyde's Comedy Club in New Orleans in 1981.

The following year, Ellen sent in a videotape of her standup act to enter a national talent contest held by the cable network Showtime. She won, earning the title of "Funniest Person in America," and was immediately launched into the national spotlight. She began traveling across the country performing her standup act, and she even began appearing in several HBO specials.

"You have to be really, really tough-skinned," Ellen said of life on the comedy road.

> There's lots of traveling, lots of being by yourself, lots of really rude drunk people. You're not just in big cities; you're in small towns, mini malls, strip malls . . . lots of places where, literally, the soup of the day got top billing. There would be a chalkboard on the sidewalk and it would say: SOUP OF THE DAY: BROCCOLI. AND ELLEN DEGENERES.

Then, in 1986, the dream she'd predicted came true. She became the first female comedian invited for a chat on Johnny Carson's couch on *The Tonight Show*.

"I had created that experience because I wanted it," Ellen said.

Ellen had to perform in a lot of comedy clubs before becoming the television star she is today.

After the career-altering event, Ellen continued her successful standup run. But she was hampered by her fears about what people would think if her sexuality were ever to become widespread knowledge.

"I started this path of stand-up, and it was successful, and it was great," she said to the crowd at Tulane. "But it was hard because I was trying to please everybody, and I had this secret that I was keeping that I was gay. And I thought that if people found out, they wouldn't like me, they wouldn't laugh at me."

Her acting career started with the 1989 Fox sitcom *Open House*, in which she played Margo Van Meter, a sparky receptionist at a Los Angeles real estate firm. "In *Open House* I was trying to be this goofy character," Ellen said. "She was so over-the-top and so weird."

She then worked on ABC's *Laurie Hill*, before being offered her own sitcom on ABC called *These Friends of Mine*. After the first season, the show, co-starring Jeremy Piven and Joely Fisher, was re-titled *Ellen*. Ellen earned Emmy nominations for Best Actress each year during the show's run from 1994 to 1998.

"I got my own sitcom, and that was very successful, another level of success," she said as she continued her reminiscing with the Tulane graduates.

Then I thought, "What if they find out I'm gay? They'll never watch." This was a long time ago. This was when we just had white presidents. But, anyway, this was back many years ago. And I finally decided that I was living with so much shame and so much fear that I just couldn't live that way anymore. And I decided to come out and make it creative, and my character would come out at the same time. And it wasn't to make a political statement. It wasn't to do anything other than to free myself up from this heaviness that I was carrying around, and I just wanted to be honest. And I thought, "What's the worst that can happen? I can lose my career." I did. I lost my career.

The groundbreaking 1997 "Puppy Episode" made headlines as 46 million people saw her character, Ellen Morgan, coming out as a lesbian to her friends, becoming the only openly gay leading character on television. Ellen earned the coveted Peabody Award, which honors distinguished achievement in television. The episode also won an Emmy for writing and remains a pivotal moment in the movement for gay rights in the United States.

"I tried to incorporate educational things about what people actually go through when they're coming out, and it wasn't funny," she said at the time. "Because it's not funny."

At the same time, Ellen also publicly came out herself. Her smiling face was featured on the cover of *Time* magazine with the headline, "Yep, I'm Gay." Many people were supportive of this bold and momentous step, and she received a special honor from the Gay and Lesbian Alliance Against Defamation. Some mainstream companies, however, pulled their advertising from the show because they felt the subject matter was too *controversial*. And

conservative Reverend Jerry Falwell re-named the brave actress "Ellen Degenerate" and publically scolded the television show.

"I didn't choose to be anything other than a comedian," Ellen said in the *Time* article. "I just happen to be gay, and I didn't feel like keeping it a secret, so I announced it. It all turned into this whole big political thing."

But despite the show's historic significance, American culture apparently wasn't ready for such a change.

"The show was cancelled after six years, without even telling me. I read it in the paper," Ellen said. "The phone didn't ring for three years. I had no offers. Nobody wanted to touch me at all."

But in spite of the frightening and uncertain time, when she had no idea where her career would end up, or if she would be back shucking oysters in New Orleans, Ellen found a silver lining. Again, she saw how her comedy had the power to touch people's lives.

"I was getting letters from kids that almost committed suicide, but didn't because of what I did," she said. "And I realized that I had a purpose. And it wasn't just about me, and it wasn't about celebrity. I felt like I was being punished. It was a bad time. I was angry, and I was sad."

After the gap in career opportunities, though, Ellen began to claw her way back. She got an offer to host a talk show. She was the voice of the forgetful fish Dory in the wildly successful Disney/Pixar animated film *Finding Nemo*. The movie grossed more than $860 million worldwide and won the Academy Award for Best Animated Feature.

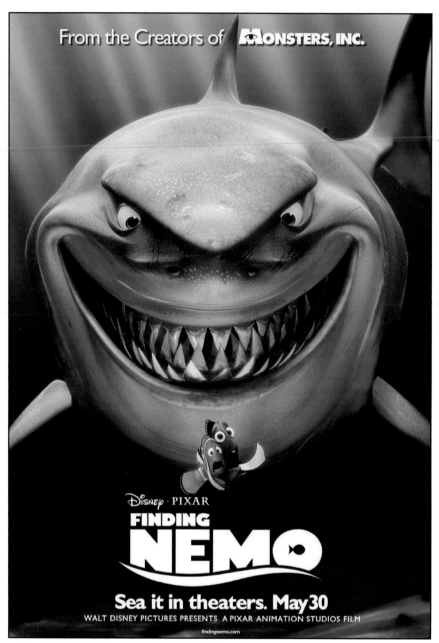

Ellen's voice acting was a big part of Finding Nemo's *success.*

"I wrote it completely with [Ellen] in mind," *Nemo* director Andrew Stanton said.

Ellen also appeared in thirty-five cities for a comedy tour called "Here and Now," which was taped for HBO and nominated for two Emmy Awards. She also wrote a pair of books, *My Point . . . And I Do Have One*, published in 1995, and *The Funny Thing Is . . .* which reached the top of the *New York Times'* best-seller list when it was released in 2003. The audio version of the book also garnered a Grammy Award nomination for Best Comedy Album in 2005.

Ellen later had a CBS sitcom called *The Ellen Show*, which ran from 2001 to 2002, in which she played another lesbian character named Ellen. "A lot of the humor on sitcoms comes from being sarcastic and mean-spirited," she said about the show. "I just have never liked that. I like things that are funny because they're silly or because they're smart."

She also appeared in feature films such as *EDTV* with Matthew McConaughey and director Ron Howard, *The Love Letter*, *Goodbye Love*, *Coneheads*, and *Mr. Wrong* with Bill Pullman.

Her show launched in September 2003, and in its first year, it earned a record twelve Daytime Emmy nominations and won four awards, including Outstanding Talk Show. In the following two years, it earned eleven more Daytime Emmys. But despite the success, many people didn't think the show would survive.

"The people that offered the talk show tried to sell it and most stations didn't want to pick it up," Ellen recalled. "Most people didn't want to buy it because they thought nobody would watch me. And, really, when I look back on it, I wouldn't change a thing."

With *The Ellen DeGeneres Show*, she was back in the national spotlight. The show became known for her fun-loving dance moves, A-list guests, and deadpan comedy. "I want the show to reach people and to be something positive," Ellen said. "[When] I lost my show, I lost my entire career, and I lost everything for three years. I got to learn that I was strong enough to start over again."

The show opened new doors for Ellen, who became a spokesperson for American Express in a global advertising campaign. Famed photographer Annie Leibovitz created the print ads. Ellen also appeared in a series of humorous TV commercials that combined her love for dancing, working, and animals, just as she had dreamed about as a child.

"It was so important for me to lose everything, because I found what the most important thing is—to be true to yourself," she said. "Ultimately, that's what's gotten me to this place. I don't live in fear. I'm free. I have no secrets. And I know I'll always be okay, because no matter what, I know who I am."

Ellen also helped others to know who they were. She received thousands more letters from gay and lesbian people all over the world. People she'd never met felt a connection to the rising star, who lived her life publicly and honestly.

"When I was younger, I thought success was something different. I thought, 'When I grow up, I want to be famous. I want to be a star. I want to be in movies. When I grow up, I want to see the world and drive nice cars'," Ellen told the graduates at Tulane University.

But my idea of success is different today. And as you grow, you'll realize the definition of success changes. . . . For me the most important thing in your life is to live your life with integrity, and not to give in to peer pressure, to try to be something that you're not. Live your life as an honest and compassionate person, to contribute in some way. . . . Follow your passion. Stay true to yourself. And never follow someone else's path.

CHAPTER 4
PRESENT-DAY LIFE

Words to Know
debut: A debut is a first appearance.
palpable: Something that is palpable can be touched or felt.

Since the launch of her show, Ellen's life has been a series of increasingly positive and exciting events, both personally and professionally. Her many contributions to the entertainment industry earned her numerous awards, including a Golden Apple Award as Female Discovery of the Year from the Hollywood Women's Press Club, a Lucy Award honoring women in television and film, as well as an Amnesty International Award. She'd come a long way from the flea-infested apartment in New Orleans!

In 2005, Ellen continued her stance as a role model to young people by speaking publicly about her sexual abuse for the first time. "It's important for teenage girls out there to hear that there are different ways to say, 'No,'" she said. "And if it ever happens to them, they should tell someone right away."

Also that year, she hosted the 57th Annual Emmy Awards, just a few weeks after Hurricane Katrina had swept through her hometown of New Orleans. She was intent on keeping the evening positive and upbeat, despite the saddening events that weighed heavily on her mind.

"This is the second time I've hosted the Emmys after a national tragedy, and I just want to say that I'm honored, because it's times like this that we really, really need laughter," she told the crowd. "And be sure to look for me next month when I host the North Korean People's Choice Awards."

But her hosting responsibilities actually turned out to be much more glamorous. In 2007, Ellen became the second woman to host the Oscars at the 79th Annual Academy awards.

"Ellen DeGeneres was born to host the Academy Awards," said Oscars Producer Laura Ziskin.

> There is no more challenging hosting job in show business. It requires someone who can keep the show alive and fresh and moving, as well as someone who is a flat-out great entertainer. Ellen completely fits the bill. I can already tell she is going to set the bar very high for herself and therefore for all of us involved in putting on the show.

The support for her role was overwhelming. "She just sparkles," said Academy President Sid Ganis. "She is such a pleasure to watch. Her wit cuts to the truth of things, but in a wonderfully warm-spirited way. I think she'll be a fantastic host for this show and we're extremely pleased that she's agreed to do it."

Ellen with the Jonas Brothers.

Ellen becoming a judge on American Idol *proved she'd become one of the biggest television stars in the country.*

Then in 2008, Ellen became the new face of CoverGirl cosmetics. She made the announcement on her talk show and struck a modeling pose. "That's the first thing they teach you when you're a CoverGirl. It's a very cool thing, I'm honored and the photo shoot was easy, breezy, beautiful . . . CoverGirl," she said, invoking the product's famous tagline.

The next year, after singer Paula Abdul left the hugely popular reality show *American Idol*, Fox Network made an announcement. "We are thrilled to have Ellen DeGeneres join the *American Idol* judges' table this season," announced Mike Darnell, President of Alternative Entertainment for FOX.

> She is truly one of America's funniest people and a fantastic performer who understands what it's like to stand up in front of audiences and entertain them every day. We feel that her vast entertainment experience—combined with her quick wit and passion for music—will add a fresh new energy to the show.

She made her *debut* on the show on February 9, 2010, joining the judging panel to critique hopeful singers in the nationwide competition.

"We're all delighted to have Ellen join our ninth season of *American Idol*," said the show's executive producer, Cecile Frot-Coutaz. "Beyond her incredible sense of humor and love of music, she brings with her an immense warmth and compassion that is almost **palpable**. She is one of America's foremost entertainers, and we cannot wait to have her join our team."

But the stint only lasted one season. Ellen realized that she wasn't a good fit for the program. "I also realized this season that while I love discovering, supporting and nurturing young talent, it was hard for me to judge people and sometimes hurt their feelings," she said.

Instead, she found another way to help up-and-coming musical talent find an outlet for their talents. She announced on her talk show in 2010 that she was starting a label called eleveneleven. Her first act was twelve-year-old Greyson Chance, a sensation on YouTube with his piano version of Lady Gaga's "Paparazzi."

"It's something I've been thinking about doing for a while," Ellen said.

In 2010, she also achieved a spot on the list of the 20 Richest Women in Entertainment, which requires a minimum net worth of $45 million. She was included in *Forbes'* Top 5 Most Influential Women in Media list and was voted Best Daytime Talk-Show Host by Parade.com readers. She also beat out such world-renowned hosts as Oprah Winfrey and Jay Leno when she was voted Favorite TV Personality in the annual Harris Poll assessment.

She was honored with *TelevisionWeek*'s Syndication Personality of the Year and voted to the top of Oxygen's 50 Funniest Women Alive special, joining comedy legends such as Carol Burnett and Lily Tomlin. She has also been included in *Time*'s 100 Most Influential People.

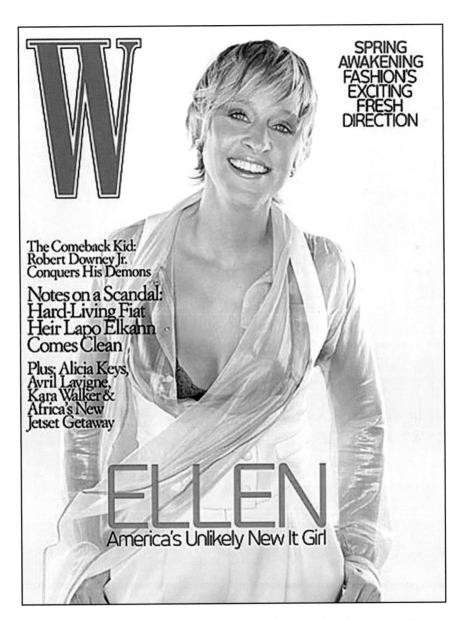

Ellen has been a comedian, actor, television host, and spokesperson. It seems there's nothing she can't do!

Ellen's work to help New Orleans after Hurricane Katrina is evidence of her commitment to sharing her success with those in need.

Personally, her life was also heading in a new direction. Ellen was using her high profile to change the lives of other people in need.

After the devastation of Hurricane Katrina, her show raised more than $10 million to improve the lives of New Orleans residents. *The Ellen DeGeneres Show* has supported numerous charities, raising more than $50 million and bringing attention to causes such as global warming, breast cancer, and animal cruelty. She has also served as a spokesperson for General Mills' breast cancer awareness initiative, Pink for the Cure, and hosted special fundraising episodes of her show to mark Breast Cancer Awareness Month.

In 2004, she fell in love with Australian actress Portia de Rossi, who had risen to fame in the United States with television roles on *Ally McBeal* and *Arrested Development*. In 2008, an historic legal decision in California, where Ellen and Portia lived together in Beverly Hills, resulted in an historic decision for the couple as well.

"This is very exciting, I gotta say," Ellen said on her talk show. "Yesterday, if you haven't heard, the California Supreme Court overturned a ban on gay marriage."

The audience gave a deafening cheer before she continued, "So I would like to say, for the first time, I am announcing I am getting married."

The audience, which included an overjoyed Portia, went crazy as Ellen's eyes welled with tears. "If I'm this emotional now just saying it, I can't imagine how that's gonna be," she quipped. "It's something that of course we've wanted to do, and we wanted it to be legal, and we're just very excited."

Ellen's marriage to Portia shows the amazing change in the United States since the time the comedian came out on her television show years ago!

Ellen and Portia wed in an intimate ceremony, attended by just nineteen guests, including Ellen's mother, Betty, and Portia's mother, Margaret, who flew in from Australia. But the impact was far more wide reaching. Millions of people saw the couple's moving wedding video when Ellen aired it on her show, and then later made it available online. The event brought the reality of same-sex love to the consciousness of Americans throughout the country. Once again Ellen was using her celebrity status to make a significant impact on the lives of ordinary people. And this time, she was changing her own life as well.

"I pray that Portia and I are together the rest of our lives," she said. "I just feel so lucky with everything in my life right now."

Ellen never went to college. But she's clearly learned the most important things in life!

WHAT CAN YOU EXPECT?

Of course not everyone who skips college is going to be a celebrity or a millionaire. But there are other more ordinary jobs out there for people who choose to go a different route from college. Here's what you can expect to make in 100 of the top-paying jobs available to someone who has only a high school diploma. (If you're not sure what any of the jobs are, look them up on the Internet to find out more about them.) Keep in mind that these are average salaries; a beginning worker will likely make much less, while someone with many more years of experience could make much more. Also, remember that wages for the same jobs vary somewhat in different parts of the country.

Position	Average Annual Salary
rotary drill operators (oil & gas)	$59,560
commercial divers	$58,060
railroad conductors & yardmasters	$54,900
chemical plant & system operators	$54,010
real estate sales agents	$53,100
subway & streetcar operators	$52,800
postal service clerks	$51,670
pile-driver operators	$51,410
railroad brake, signal & switch operators	$49,600

brickmasons & blockmasons	$49,250
postal service mail carriers	$48,940
gaming supervisors	$48,920
postal service mail sorters & processors	$48,260
gas compressor & gas pumping station operators	$47,860
roof bolters (mining)	$47,750
forest fire fighters	$47,270
private detectives & investigators	$47,130
tapers	$46,880
continuous mining machine operators	$46,680
rail car repairers	$46,430
shuttle car operators	$46,400
rail-track laying & maintenance equipment operators	$46,000
chemical equipment operators & tenders	$45,100
explosives workers (ordnance handling experts & blasters)	$45,030
makeup artists (theatrical & performance)	$45,010
sheet metal workers	$44,890
managers/supervisors of landscaping & groundskeeping workers	$44,080
loading machine operators (underground mining)	$43,970
rough carpenters	$43,640

derrick operators (oil & gas)	$43,590
flight attendants	$43,350
refractory materials repairers (except brickmasons)	$43,310
production, planning & expediting clerks	$43,260
mine cutting & channeling machine operators	$43,120
fabric & apparel patternmakers	$42,940
service unit operators (oil, gas, & mining)	$42,690
tile & marble setters	$42,450
paperhangers	$42,310
bridge & lock tenders	$41,630
hoist & winch operators	$41,620
carpet installers	$41,560
pump operators (except wellhead pumpers)	$41,490
terrazzo workers & finishers	$41,360
plasterers & stucco masons	$41,260
painters (transportation equipment)	$41,220
automotive body & related repairers	$41,020
hazardous materials removal workers	$40,270
bailiffs	$40,240
wellhead pumpers	$40,210
maintenance workers (machinery)	$39,570
truck drivers (heavy & tractor-trailer)	$39,260

floor layers (except carpet, wood & hard tiles)	$39,190
managers of retail sales workers	$39,130
cargo & freight agents	$38,940
metal-refining furnace operators & tenders	$38,830
excavating & loading machine and dragline operators	$38,540
separating, filtering, clarifying & still machine operators	$38,450
motorboat operators	$38,390
dredge operators	$38,330
lay-out workers (metal & plastic)	$38,240
forest fire inspectors & prevention specialists	$38,180
medical & clinical laboratory technicians	$37,860
tire builders	$37,830
dental laboratory technicians	$37,690
paving, surfacing & tamping equipment operators	$37,660
locksmiths & safe repairers	$37,550
sailors & marine oilers	$37,310
dispatchers (except police, fire & ambulance)	$37,310
pipelayers	$37,040
helpers (extraction workers)	$36,870

rolling machine setters, operators & tenders	$36,670
welders, cutters & welder fitters	$36,630
solderers & brazers	$36,630
gem & diamond workers	$36,620
police, fire & ambulance dispatchers	$36,470
models	$36,420
meter readers (utilities)	$36,400
mechanical door repairers	$36,270
public address system & other announcers	$36,130
rail yard engineers, dinkey operators & hostlers	$36,090
bus drivers (transit & intercity)	$35,990
insurance policy processing clerks	$35,740
insurance claims clerks	$35,740
computer-controlled machine tool operators (metal and plastic)	$35,570
license clerks	$35,570
court clerks	$35,570
fallers	$35,570
septic tank servicers & sewer pipe cleaners	$35,470
parking enforcement workers	$35,360
highway maintenance workers	$35,310
floor sanders & finishers	$35,140

tool grinders, filers, & sharpeners	$35,110
paper goods machine setters, operators & tenders	$35,040
printing machine operators	$35,030
inspectors, testers, sorters, samplers & weighers	$34,840
pourers & casters (metal)	$34,760
loan interviewers & clerks	$34,670
furnace, kiln, oven, drier & kettle operators & tenders	$34,410
recreational vehicle service technicians	$34,320
roustabouts (oil & gas)	$34,190

Source: Bureau of Labor Statistics, U.S. Department of Labor, 2008.

Find Out More

In Books

DeGeneres, Betty. *Just a Mom*. Los Angeles: Alyson Books, 2000.

DeGeneres, Ellen. *My Point…And I Do Have One*. New York: Bantam, 2007.

___. *The Funny Thing Is…*. New York: Simon & Schuster, 2004.

Seba, Jaime A. *Coming Out: Telling Family and Friends*. Philadelphia: Mason Crest Publishers, 2011.

Sharp, Katie. *Ellen Degeneres (People in the News)*. Farmington Hills, Minn: Lucent, 2010.

On the Internet

Biography
www.notablebiographies.com/news/Ca-Ge/DeGeneres-Ellen.html

The Ellen DeGeneres Show
ellen.warnerbros.com

Ellen Quotes
www.quotationspage.com/quotes/Ellen_DeGeneres/

New Orleans
www.neworleansonline.com

Portia de Rossi
loveportia.org

DISCLAIMER

Index

Picture Credits

About the Author

Jaime A. Seba's studied political science at Syracuse University before switching her focus to communications. She has worked both in New York and on the West Coast as an activist for LGBT awareness. She is currently a freelance writer based in Seattle.